Escape the Sting!

DEADLY ANIMALS

by Alex Hall

Minneapolis, Minnesota

Credits
Cover and title page, © Lauren Suryanata/Shutterstock; 4TL, © Twin Chan/Adobe Stock; 4B, © Frank Reiser/Shutterstock; 5M, © apple2499/Adobe Stock; 5MR, © nitinan/Adobe Stock; 6, © Dustin Rhoades/Shutterstock; 7, © asbtkb/Adobe Stock; 8, © Andres Nunez Mora/Adobe Stock; 9, © Wirestock/Adobe Stock; 10, © Picture Partners/Adobe Stock; 11, © Dancestrokes/Shutterstock; 12, © Francisco Farriols Sarabia/Wikimedia; 13, © Sol Quipildor/Wikimedia; 14, © akiyoko/Shutterstock; 15, © ThomasLENNE/Adobe Stock; 16, © Vinicius R. Souza/Shutterstock; 17, © robertharding/Alamy Stock Photo; 18, © Laura Dts/Shutterstock; 19, © Joe Belanger/Shutterstock; 20, © Protasov AN/Shutterstock; 21, © Agus Gatam/Adobe Stock; 22, © Andriy Nekrasov/Shutterstock; 23, © "Marc Henauer/Nitrogenic Photography"/Adobe Stock; 24, © Visual&&Written SL/Alamy Stock Photo; 25, © Gary Bell/ Oceanwide/Minden Pictures; 26, © JENG BO YUAN/Shutterstock; 27, © mirecca/Adobe Stock; 28, © Gary Bell/ Oceanwide/Minden Pictures; 29, © Gary Bell/ Oceanwide/Minden Pictures; 30TL, © Apchanel/Adobe Stock; 30B, © Ian Redding/Adobe Stock

Bearport Publishing Company Product Development Team
Publisher: Jen Jenson; Director of Product Development: Spencer Brinker; Editorial Director: Allison Juda; Editor: Cole Nelson; Editor: Tiana Tran; Production Editor: Naomi Reich; Art Director: Kim Jones; Designer: Kayla Eggert; Designer: Steve Scheluchin; Production Specialist: Owen Hamlin

Library of Congress Cataloging-in-Publication Data is available at www.loc.gov or upon request from the publisher.

ISBN: 979-8-89577-088-7 (hardcover)
ISBN: 979-8-89577-531-8 (paperback)
ISBN: 979-8-89577-205-8 (ebook)

© 2026 BookLife Publishing
This edition is published by arrangement with BookLife Publishing.

North American adaptations © 2026 Bearport Publishing Company. All rights reserved. No part of this publication may be reproduced in whole or in part, stored in any retrieval system, or transmitted in any form or by any means, electronic, mechanical, photocopying, recording, or otherwise, without written permission from the publisher. Bearport Publishing is a division of FlutterBee Education Group.

For more information, write to Bearport Publishing, 3500 American Blvd W, Suite 150, Bloomington, MN 55431.

Contents

A World of Killer Critters 4
Animals Sting! 6
Bullet Ant 8
Honeybee 10
Executioner Wasp 12
Northern Giant Hornet 14
Tarantula Hawk Wasp 16
Cone Snail 18
Deathstalker Scorpion 20
Stonefish 22
Australian Box Jellyfish 24
Stingray 26
The Deadliest Sting! 28
Critters Everywhere 30
Glossary 31
Index 32
Read More 32
Learn More Online 32

A World of Killer Critters

The world is full of wonderful, wild, and dangerous critters! Animals everywhere have lots of different ways to defend themselves or catch a tasty meal.

Whether an animal looks cozy or killer, it's best to watch out! It might just sting, bite, claw, or squeeze you when you least expect it.

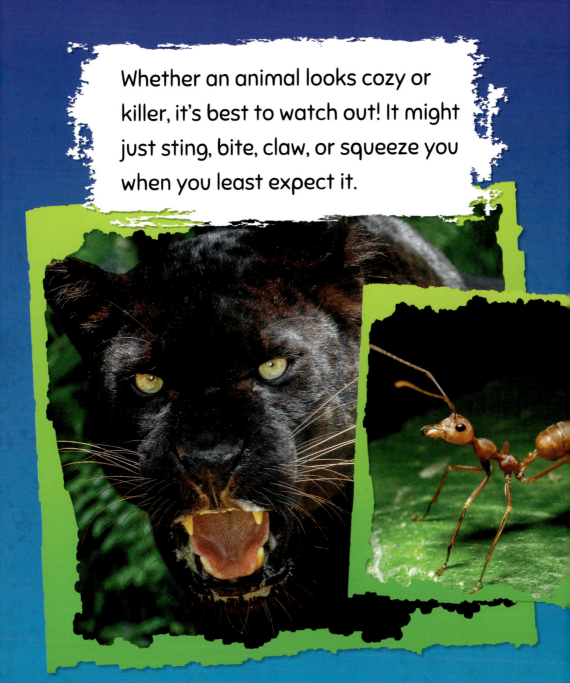

READ ON TO LEARN MORE ABOUT SOME OF THE WORLD'S SCARIEST STINGING ANIMALS . . . IF YOU DARE!

Animals Sting!

One of the ways animals stay safe or catch their next meal is to sting. *ZIP!* But what makes an animal's sting so dangerous?

Some animals have sharp stingers on their bodies. They use them to **inject** deadly **venom** into their **prey**.

Animal stings can be dangerous in different ways. They pass on venom that can cause sickness, numbness, or even stop a beating heart! And what makes all this stinging even scarier? It can kill within minutes!

Let's take a look at some killer critters and score their dangerous stings. We'll rate their damage and pain, how fast they move, and their venomous effects. Which animal will win this deadly competition?

Bullet Ant

The first competitor is the bullet ant. This **insect** was named for its unpleasant sting. People compare the stinging pain to being hit by a bullet. *BANG!*

The bullet ant's stinger is located near its rear end. The critter uses its stinger to defend itself and to hunt.

A sting from the bullet ant is considered the most painful of any insect. This attack is strong enough to kill insects. While it's not as deadly against humans, it can **paralyze** parts of a person's body.

KILLER CRITTER SCORECARD

PAIN FACTOR	6
VENOM DANGER	4
BODY DAMAGE	6
CREATURE SPEED	3

BULLET ANT

TOTAL 19

Honeybee

When you think of stingers, honeybees might come to mind. These insects play an important role as **pollinators**. But they are also known to pack a punch.

Honeybees don't sting at random. That's because they die after using their stingers. So, honeybees use this kind of attack only to defend themselves or their **colonies**.

Most honeybees aren't as deadly as they appear. They are only a real problem for people with bee **allergies**. Luckily, there are medicines to stop the venom.

KILLER CRITTER SCORECARD

⚡ PAIN FACTOR	3	
💧 VENOM DANGER	2	
🧍 BODY DAMAGE	2	
⏱ CREATURE SPEED	5	

HONEYBEE

TOTAL
12

Executioner Wasp

The executioner wasp is one of the largest wasps in South America. This yellow-and-brown insect has a nasty sting. Get too close and you might feel its wrath.

When hunting, the executioner wasp quickly paralyzes an insect with its stinger. Death soon follows. Then, the wasp drags its meal back home to feed its growing babies.

One sting from an executioner wasp can leave a person in pain for almost a week. Luckily, its sting is not enough to cause deadly harm ... unless you're allergic.

KILLER CRITTER SCORECARD

EXECUTIONER WASP

PAIN FACTOR	8
VENOM DANGER	3
BODY DAMAGE	6
CREATURE SPEED	5

TOTAL 22

Northern Giant Hornet

The fearsome northern giant hornet was originally found in Asia but soon moved to parts of North America. This insect is sometimes referred to as the murder hornet.

Northern giant hornets sometimes hunt in groups. After finding a beehive, they will crawl inside and attack. *RIP!* These hornets rip the heads, wings, and legs off honeybees until they kill the whole hive.

For humans, a sting from the northern giant hornet is more toxic than that of a honeybee. And unlike a bee, this hornet can sting more than once. The northern giant hornet's stinger is even strong enough to go through a beekeeper's suit!

KILLER CRITTER SCORECARD

NORTHERN GIANT HORNET

PAIN FACTOR	8
VENOM DANGER	3
BODY DAMAGE	5
CREATURE SPEED	4

TOTAL 20

Tarantula Hawk Wasp

Is it a tarantula? Is it a hawk? It's neither! The tarantula hawk wasp is a wasp that hunts spiders! The mother wasp hunts down tarantulas to feed her young.

First, the wasp paralyzes a tarantula with its sting. Then, the killer insect lays an egg on its prey. *CRACK!* Within days, the baby wasp hatches and eats the prey alive.

Tarantula hawk wasp stings are very painful for humans. Luckily, the pain lasts for only a few minutes. Most people who aren't allergic to the sting make it out alive.

KILLER CRITTER SCORECARD

TARANTULA HAWK WASP

PAIN FACTOR	5
VENOM DANGER	2
BODY DAMAGE	4
CREATURE SPEED	3

TOTAL 14

Cone Snail

The slimy cone snail sits and waits in shallow water close to a **coral reef**. Don't let its colorful shell fool you! This critter does not like to be touched.

While slow-moving, this critter still manages to catch small fish and worms. The cone snail can paralyze its prey with a single powerful sting from a venom-filled tooth.

Despite its small size, the cone snail is one of the most venomous ocean **predators**. For humans, one sting can cause **muscle** paralysis, trouble breathing, and even death.

KILLER CRITTER SCORECARD

CONE SNAIL

PAIN FACTOR	6
VENOM DANGER	4
BODY DAMAGE	7
CREATURE SPEED	2

TOTAL 19

Deathstalker Scorpion

Watch your feet! There are many scorpions living in the harsh deserts of Asia and Africa. But when it comes to the deadliest, the deathstalker scorpion comes out on top.

Hiding under rocks allows the deathstalker scorpion to take its prey by surprise. First, it grabs the small insect with its powerful pincers. Then, the scorpion quickly stings its prey before the critter can run away.

When humans are stung, the scorpion's venom can lead to heart or breathing problems. The venom can sometimes be strong enough to be deadly to young people and the elderly.

KILLER CRITTER SCORECARD

DEATHSTALKER SCORPION

PAIN FACTOR	4
VENOM DANGER	6
BODY DAMAGE	7
CREATURE SPEED	6

TOTAL 23

Stonefish

The stonefish blends in with its rocky home, sitting perfectly still on the sea floor. While the critter may not look dangerous, it is actually the most venomous fish in the world.

Using their rock-like appearance to blend in, stonefish patiently wait for prey to come to them. Then, they use their strong jaws and big mouths to swallow their meals whole.

Watch your step, because one wrong move could be your last! The stonefish has spines on its body that inject a deadly venom. This venom can cause paralysis and heart failure. And for some humans, it can kill within an hour!

KILLER CRITTER SCORECARD

STONEFISH

PAIN FACTOR	7
VENOM DANGER	4
BODY DAMAGE	6
CREATURE SPEED	1

TOTAL 18

Australian Box Jellyfish

There are many different types of box jellyfish. The Australian box jellyfish is the deadliest and most venomous of them all. A sting from this jelly can leave a nasty scar. That is, if you live to tell the tale.

The Australian box jellyfish has tentacles that contain special stinging cells with little needles. The jelly launches these poison-filled needles into its prey.

The pain from an Australian box jelly's sting can cause people to go into shock and drown. Some have heart failure and die within minutes. If a person survives an attack, the pain from the box jelly's sting can last for weeks.

KILLER CRITTER SCORECARD

AUSTRALIAN BOX JELLYFISH

PAIN FACTOR	10
VENOM DANGER	9
BODY DAMAGE	7
CREATURE SPEED	2

TOTAL: 28

Stingray

As its name suggests, the stingray is known for its powerful sting. The long, flat fish is often found swimming in warm tropical waters.

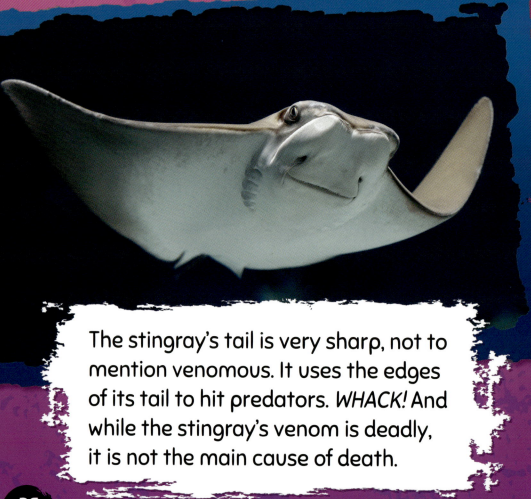

The stingray's tail is very sharp, not to mention venomous. It uses the edges of its tail to hit predators. WHACK! And while the stingray's venom is deadly, it is not the main cause of death.

The force of a stingray's sting is strong enough to tear through bodies. The small spines on its tail cut skin, which may cause swelling and pain that lasts for days.

KILLER CRITTER SCORECARD

PAIN FACTOR	7
VENOM DANGER	6
BODY DAMAGE	6
CREATURE SPEED	3

STINGRAY

TOTAL
22

The Deadliest Sting!

Who comes out on top in this killer critter competition? The Australian box jellyfish wins!

While this jelly isn't the fastest moving animal in the competition, its scary stingers and killer venom make it the deadly winner.

Venom from these jellies contains toxins that can attack a person's heart and **nervous system**. A victim may die within five minutes!

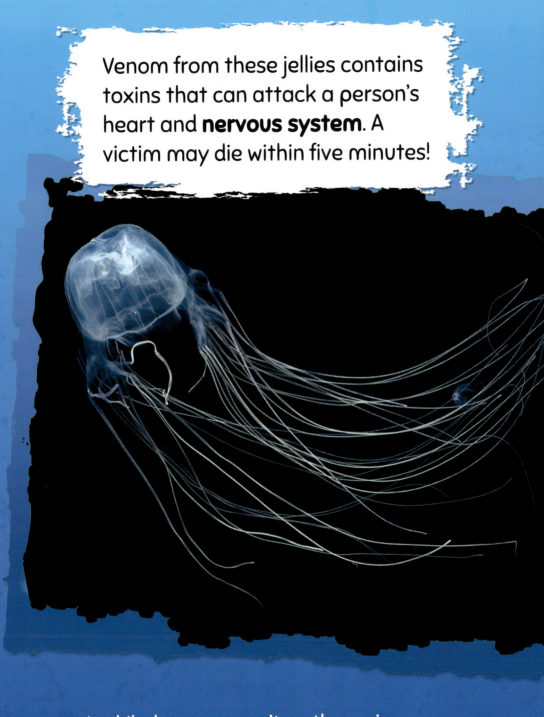

Luckily, humans aren't on the main menu for Australian box jellies. Still, don't get too close to these critters either!

Critters Everywhere

The world is a big place, full of amazing animals. But the next time you see a wild critter, stay back. It might have a powerful jaw, a venomous stinger, or a sharp tail!

Glossary

allergies medical conditions that cause people to become sick after eating, touching, or breathing something

colonies groups of animals living in one place

coral reef a group of rocklike structures formed from the skeletons of sea animals called coral polyps

inject to push a liquid into something using a needlelike object

insect an animal with six legs, three body parts, and an exoskeleton

muscle a part of the body that helps it move

nervous system the complex body system that carries messages between the brain and the rest of the body

paralyze to cause a body part to lose feeling and the ability to move

pollinators animals that spread pollen from flower to flower so that the flowers can make seeds

predators animals that hunt and eat other animals

prey animals that are hunted and eaten by other animals

venom a harmful substance that is injected through a bite or a sting

Index

babies 12, 16
coral reefs 18
deserts 20
jaws 22, 30
medicines 11
oceans 19
pincers 20
scars 24
shells 18
spines 23, 27
stingers 6, 8, 10, 12, 15, 28, 30
tails 26–27, 30

Read More

Beer, Julie. *Bite, Sting, Kill: The Incredible Science of Toxins, Venom, Fangs & Stingers.* Washington, D.C.: National Geographic Kids, 2023.

Loh-Hagan, Virginia. *Stinging Animals (Weird Animal Science: The Breakdown).* Ann Arbor, MI: 45th Parallel Press, 2025.

Rose, Rachel. *Australian Box Jellyfish (Danger Down Under).* Minneapolis: Bearport Publishing Company, 2024.

Learn More Online

1. Go to **FactSurfer.com** or scan the QR code below.
2. Enter **"Escape Sting"** into the search box.
3. Click on the cover of this book to see a list of websites.